D1402621

DATE DUE

JUN 1 0 1996	SEP 2 0 2003	
JUL 1 2 1996	NOV 0 7 2003	
SEP 1 0 1997	JUL 2 9 2008	
MAR 1 9 1998		
JUL 3 1 1998		
APR 0 9 1999		
JUN 2 4 1999		
APR 1 0 2000		

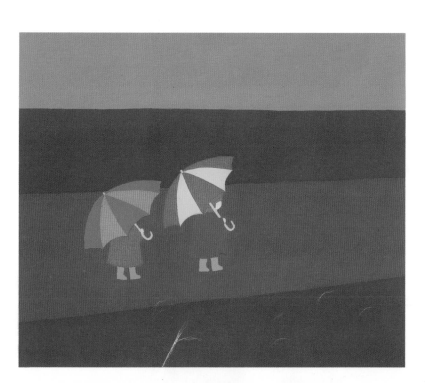

Seasons

Seasons

Heidi Goennel

Little, Brown and Company
Boston   Toronto

First Edition

Library of Congress Cataloging-in-Publication Data
Goennel, Heidi.
    Seasons.

    Summary: Highlights the moods of the four seasons, depicting
such activities as snowball fights and kite flying.
    1. Seasons—Juvenile literature. 2. Play—Juvenile literature.
[1. Seasons] I. Title
QH81.G55 1986   574.5'43   85-31226
ISBN 0-316-31836-1

DNP

Published simultaneously in Canada
by Little, Brown & Company (Canada) Limited

Printed in Japan

To Peter

Seasons change throughout the year. Spring becomes summer, fall becomes winter. I love the special way each season makes me feel. But mostly I love all the different things there are to do.

Spring is warm and gentle.

I love to splash in puddles

To pick fresh flowers

And see new baby animals

But mostly I love to fly my kite.

Summer is hot and lazy.

I love to go barefoot outdoors

To eat ice cream cones

And daydream all day long

But mostly I love to go to the beach.

Fall is cool and crisp.

I love to pick pumpkins

To jump in the leaves

And go back to school

But mostly I love to go trick-or-treating.

Winter is cold and clean.

I love to take walks on a starry night

To curl up in a cozy chair

And send a secret valentine

But mostly I love to play in the snow.

Seasons change throughout the year. I love watching the seasons come and go, and knowing they'll come back year after year.